# Menorca
*Travel Guide*

*Quick Trips Series*

No part of this publication may be reproduced, stored in a retrieval system, or transmitted, in any form or by any means without the prior written permission of the publisher, nor be otherwise circulated in any form of binding or cover other than that in which it is published and without similar condition being imposed on the subsequent purchaser. If there are any errors or omissions in copyright acknowledgements the publisher will be pleased to insert the appropriate acknowledgement in any subsequent printing of this publication. Although we have taken all reasonable care in researching this book we make no warranty about the accuracy or completeness of its content and disclaim all liability arising from its use.

Copyright © 2016, Astute Press
All Rights Reserved.

# Table of Contents

## MENORCA — 5
- CUSTOMS & CULTURE ... 8
- GEOGRAPHY ... 10
- WEATHER & BEST TIME TO VISIT ... 11

## SIGHTS & ACTIVITIES: WHAT TO SEE & DO — 14
- MAHON ... 14
- MAHON HARBOUR BOAT TRIPS ... 15
- NECROPOLIS CAVES (CALAS COVES) ... 17
- BINIBECA BEACH ... 18
- MOUNT TORO ... 19
- CIUTADELLA ... 20
- MENORCA CATHEDRAL, CIUTADELLA ... 21
- SON CATLAR PREHISTORIC SITE ... 22
- TORRETRENCADA ... 23
- SAN AGUEDA CASTLE ... 24

## BUDGET TIPS — 26
- ACCOMMODATION ... 26

    Hotel Mar Blava ................................................................................27
    Hotel Hesperia Menorca Patricia........................................................28
    Apartamentos Roc Lago Park ............................................................30
    Hotel Globales Almirante Farragut .....................................................31
    Hostal Jume ......................................................................................32
🌐 SHOPPING ............................................................................**33**
    Castillo Menorca................................................................................35
    Mercat de Claustre ............................................................................35
    Centro Artesanal ...............................................................................36
    Bangels Accessories ........................................................................37
    Arts & Crafts Markets ........................................................................38
🌐 PLACES TO EAT ...................................................................**39**
    La Minerva........................................................................................40
    Bar Restaurant España .....................................................................41
    Restaurante Ca Na Marga ................................................................42
    Cafe Balear ......................................................................................43
    La Cayena ........................................................................................43

# KNOW BEFORE YOU GO     45

🌐 **ENTRY REQUIREMENTS** .....................................................45

🌐 **HEALTH INSURANCE**..........................................................45

🌐 **TRAVELLING WITH PETS**....................................................46

🌐 **AIRPORTS**..........................................................................47

🌐 **AIRLINES** ...........................................................................48

🌐 **CURRENCY**........................................................................49

🌐 **BANKING & ATMS** ..............................................................49

🌐 **CREDIT CARDS** .................................................................49

🌐 **TOURIST TAXES**................................................................50

🌐 **RECLAIMING VAT** ..............................................................50

🌐 **TIPPING POLICY**................................................................51

🌐 **MOBILE PHONES** ...............................................................52

- 🌐 Dialling Code .................................................................. 53
- 🌐 Emergency Numbers ....................................................... 53
- 🌐 Public Holidays ............................................................... 53
- 🌐 Time Zone ........................................................................ 54
- 🌐 Daylight Savings Time ..................................................... 55
- 🌐 School Holidays .............................................................. 55
- 🌐 Trading Hours ................................................................. 55
- 🌐 Driving Laws ................................................................... 56
- 🌐 Drinking Laws ................................................................. 56
- 🌐 Smoking Laws ................................................................. 57
- 🌐 Electricity ......................................................................... 57
- 🌐 Food & Drink ................................................................... 58

# **MENORCA TRAVEL GUIDE**

## Menorca

Menorca (also known as Minorca) is one of the most beautiful islands in the Mediterranean. One of the Spanish Balearic Islands, Menorca is known for its quiet ambience, golden beaches and sparkling oceans.

This island off the coast of mainland Spain may look just a little bit too laid back, but this is a mischaracterisation

# MENORCA TRAVEL GUIDE

and you will find a wealth of activities and interesting places to keep even the most demanding tourist happy.

Indeed, the vibe is far more relaxed than other commercial islands, and this grants you the opportunity to indulge in all your favorite activities at leisure.

It is a popular destination among sporting types and boasts some of the best diving spots in the entire Mediterranean. The island is dotted with secret areas and sheltered coves that play home to the nightingales. Their fabled songs can be heard echoing through the island in the warm spring and summer months. It is of little wonder that Menorca is quickly gaining popularity as the destination for young couples and families.

When coming to Menorca, visitors seek sun, sea and sand, and the island will not disappoint. An ancient city is surrounded and cradled by imposing cliffs, white beaches, sweeping fields and woody ravines. This jewel of the Balearic Islands is a place of contrast, of remote beaches and vibrant city life, of relaxing and indulging.

# MENORCA TRAVEL GUIDE

Menorca's greatest appeal lies in its beaches, with over 100 beaches to choose from. Nude bathing is still commonplace at many beaches, but the practice thereof is technically illegal. Going for the pleasant weather, hearty food and beaches alone is reason enough to visit Menorca. However, it is its rich heritage and ancient history of a lifetime of invasions that invites travelers to explore its secrets.

Commanding one of the best and strategic natural harbour positions this side of the Med, people settled on the island as early as 4000BC. Thanks to this strategic and popular position, Menorca has seen its fair share of upheaval.

The first inhabitants are believed to Spaniards from the Neolithic era, and their decedents build the monolithic structures that we see to this day scattered around the island. The island range was furthermore frequented by Barbary Pirates from the Americas, resulting in the many watchtowers and fortifications that are still standing

No doubt these invasions helped to shape the current state of affairs. Modern day Menorca is completely self-sufficient and independent. It does not rely solely on tourism, as it has a booming industry of its own. Handmade leatherwork, costume jewelry and even locally manufactured gin will make a fine souvenir.

In spite of its increasing popularity, Menorca remains essentially unspoilt, maintaining its Spanish charm and welcoming temperament.

## 🌐 Customs & Culture

The richness of the culture is mainly due to the said strategic and central position of the island in the heart of the Med. Traditions were greatly shaped by the invasions and colonisations since explores first discovered its shores.

Locals speak a dialect of Catalan, a colorful language that has its roots in Arab and French, with a British influence. In contrast, the architecture is strongly Moor inspired, as

# MENORCA TRAVEL GUIDE

can be seen in the white washed houses and complicated cistern systems.

As is customary in a predominantly Spanish culture, warm hospitality and chivalry is at the order of the day, and it is very common to acknowledge and greet the people you meet. And best not forget about the time honoured custom of the midday siesta that is still practiced in many areas. Locals are a jovial bunch, and this afternoon nap enables them to fully enjoy their evenings. Here, people will rarely dine out before 10.00pm.

Dating back to the times of the invasions, landowners kept Berber horses in order to defend the island from invaders, and these strong equestrian traditions are observed all over the island. Menorcans are fiercely proud of their powerful and spirited horses, famed for their beauty and speed. Races are a favourite pastime of many, with weekly events and fiesta taking place is both Ciutadella and Mao.

# MENORCA TRAVEL GUIDE

Locals love a good merrymaking, paired with a passion for concocting simple but scrumptious culinary delights. Most of the dishes are prepared from local ingredients, with a strong focus on seafood, cheese and locally produced fresh produce. You might say that gin is the national drink, as it is distilled on the island from grapes, and flavoured with juniper.

## 🌐 Geography

The island is located right in the heart of the western Mediterranean of the West Coast of Spain, but lies almost halfway between Marseille in France, and Algiers in Algeria.

Menorca is also referred to as "The Quiet One" out of the Balearic Islands, as party goers tend to favour the neighbouring island of Ibiza. With a current population of roughly 68 000 inhabitants, Menorca has undergone very little commercial changes. It has resisted full-blown urbanization and kept itself sheltered from the effects that come with mass development.

# MENORCA TRAVEL GUIDE

Still, it is the second largest island the Balearic range, but with more beaches than Majorca and Ibiza put together, and with 216 kilometers of pristine coastline, it is hardly surprising. Menorca covers a total area of 700 square kilometres, with only 47 kilometers between the main towns of Ciutadella and Mao.

Es Castell is the last town on the far eastern side, and is the first to see the sun rise. The capital of Mahon (also called Mao) is also located on the eastern side, overlooking the infamous port from a great rocky outcrop. In contrast, the northern part is rugged and rocky, with small red beach and stark cliff faces. Sparse vegetation here is encouraged by the powerful Tramuntana wind.

## 🌍 Weather & Best Time to Visit

Menorca enjoys a temperate climate throughout the year thanks mostly to its proximity to the Med. The weather is classically warm and dry during summer, with roughly 300 days of sunshine per year, and mild winters.

# **MENORCA TRAVEL GUIDE**

The average temperature usually remains at a very agreeable 17 degrees Celsius, but can climb well into the thirties in mid-summer months. Thankfully, the cooling sea breeze will see that you are never uncomfortably hot for too long. The summer months from June to September sees little to no rain, whereas the winters are typically cool and moist.

Each season on the island has something unique to offer travelers. The cooler moist periods are quiet and out of season, so it is ideal for visitors who which to escape the hustle and bustle of tourist hot spots. Spring is a wonderful time to visit, as the island explodes with life and songs of the nightingale. Sea temperatures can still be a little nippy this time of year though, so prepare yourself for a bracing dip, if you dare.

Be aware of the strong Tramontana wind in the northern region, especially in March, unless you are in the mood for a windy holiday. The islanders actually have names for all the winds, and harness its power as renewable energy sources.

# **MENORCA TRAVEL GUIDE**

For a live weather update, see:

http://www.holiday-weather.com/menorca/

# MENORCA TRAVEL GUIDE

## Sights & Activities: What to See & Do

# 🌍 Mahon

The capital, Mahon (Mao) is a picturesque and charming little town filled with local culture by day and a pumping nightlife. The tiny streets are crammed with 18th century mansions and hide interesting shops and intimate

## MENORCA TRAVEL GUIDE

restaurants where you can easily wile away a lazy afternoon.

The architecture is British-colonial inspired, and the oldest building, Arch de San Roque, dates back to the early 1600's.

While in Mahon, be sure to visit Placa de s'Eplanda, a very lively square over weekends. Be on the lookout for the Franco War Memorial and the original British Barracks. As it proper befitting to an ancient city, an old church completes the picture. The Church of Santa Maria is worth a visit, if only to see the massive organ with more than 3 000 pipes.

Let's not forget one of the world's largest natural harbours at a whopping three miles long, right here in Mahon. And what better way to explore the Port of Mahon than by boat?

# MENORCA TRAVEL GUIDE

# Mahon Harbour Boat Trips

At the harbor, you can hop on one of the many traditional boats and explore the ports and coves at leisure. The Balearic Islands boasts the cleanest water found along any coast, and this is not a mere empty promise.

One of the attractive options is the Yellow Menorcan Catamarans. These boasts are impossible to miss, and will sail the full stretch of the harbour. A single trip should take up an hour and a half and will explore all the sights of the surrounding isles and forts. The guides are extremely knowledgeable and provide valuable commentary on the run. Catamarans are equipped with a well stocked bar, and a glass floor on the lower deck lets you see right to seabed.

Trips depart roughly every four minutes from the port, but they operate only during the peak seasons of April to October.

Another popular trip is the glass bottom boats from El Pirata Azul. They act as water taxis between Mahon and neighbouring towns, and also offer longer historic tours of the ports. Trips can be tailor-made according to your needs, and different fixed trips become available every day. El Pirata Azul can be contacted at 971 367 017 or alternatively at 610 904 381.

## 🌎 Necropolis Caves (Calas Coves)

Menorca is known for its archaeological findings, but it was the discovery of Necropolis Caves got people talking. For those with a taste of the macabre, the Necropolis Caves, commonly referred to as Calas Coves, is an absolute must see.

These caves were dug out in the rocky cliff face of the Son Domingo Gorge, and can be reached from Sant Climent. As the name so aptly suggests, the necropolis hides hundreds of ancient burial sites dating back to about 1200 BC.

There are fourteen caves in total, some of which are divided into multiple rooms and supported by columns. Tombs from the Bronze Age are easily recognizable in their basic design, while the burial chambers from the Iron Age are much more complex with pillars, doorways and even outside patios.

The most impressive of the lot are the "coves de forn" with its large underground temple and façade of motifs classic to its time.

## 🌎 Binibeca Beach

Recognized as the 3 kilometre stretch of unspoilt beach, Binibeca Beach lies in the Binibequer district not far from Mahon. It is mostly a residential area with a few hotels and holiday homes

Even by Menorcan standards, Binibeca is considered to be quiet. If it is pulsating nightlife and the daily bustle that you are after, give it a skip. But if you are looking for a beach to relax and soak up the surroundings, this is the place to stop at.

In Cala Torret, one of the two districts in Binebeca, there is a supermarket and several very cosy restaurants that

# MENORCA TRAVEL GUIDE

overlook the ocean. For a place off the beaten track, the food is unpretentious but surprisingly good.

A kilometre outside of town you will find yourself in the fishing village, Binibeca Vell, which is slightly livelier, with pretty whitewashed buildings, pedestrian streets and a few more shops and restaurants than the beach area.

## Mount Toro

En-route to Ciutadella from Mahon, Mount Toro dominates the skyline at 358 meters, the highest vantage point in Menorca.

A trip to this 17th century sanctuary is an absolute must for both its insight of into past and present day culture that shaped its religion and the panoramic 360 degree view of the island. On a clear day, you can even spot the neighboring island of Mallorca in the distance.

The summit is reached by a steep winding road that gradually takes you higher as the views leave you breathless. At the apex, there is an old Augustinian monastery and a modest little Renaissance church. However, the focal point is the large statue of Christ that very much reminds of Christ the Redeemer found in Rio.

Parts of the monastery are still in use today by a community of nuns, the Franciscan Sisters of Mercy. It is a place of spiritual importance, and legend states that Mount Toro got is name from the bull (toro in Spanish) which led a group of monks to a hidden statue of the Virgin Mary in the face of the rocks.

## 🌎 Ciutadella

Located on the temperate west coast of the island, Ciutadella is the hub of the café society, where you can take time to simply relax and watch the world go by.

It is well known for their catch of the day fresh seafood, pristine beaches and annual festivals.

The largest and most popular festival is the "Festes de Sant Ciutadella" which takes place on the 23rd and 24th of

# MENORCA TRAVEL GUIDE

June. If you happen to find yourself in the city during this time, the festival is not to be missed. It is a lively affair, with jousting in the streets, colourful processions, horse racing and in typical Menorcan style, gin in abundance.

The city was once the capital on Menorca up to the British occupation, and the historic significance can been seen all around. In fact, the entire Old Quarter has been declared a National Historical Monument. Winding streets will let visitors discover the ancient Moor and Medieval history. The 17th century defence tower, Castell Sant Nicolas is worth a special mention, as it offers a breath-taking vantage point to see the sun set lazily over the Mediterranean

## 🌎 Menorca Cathedral, Ciutadella

The Menorca Cathedral in Ciutadella deserves its own entry. Originally a mosque, it was constructed as a cathedral in 1287 when Alfonso III defeated the Moors and claimed the island in the name of Christianity. It is still one of the oldest and largest buildings on the island.

Today, the style is distinctly Catalan Gothic with six chapels and numerous vaults that stir the imagination. The Chapel of Animes has a more recent Baroque influence as the cathedral changed its face in accordance with the passing centuries.

A Neo-Gothic canopy crowns the main altar, and the details, from stained glass, stone carvings and strange, mythical creatures is exquisite. In true gothic style, a large collection of gargoyles stand guard on the perimeter, and from the outside, the cathedral as quite a fortress like appearance.

## 🌐 Son Catlar Prehistoric Site

Son Catlar is another prehistoric site of great historical importance. What distinguishes it from the rest of the sites is the fact that is the only remaining ancient town in the Balearic Islands with its 900 meter defence wall still intact.

The settlement dates back to the Bronze Age, and was protected by series of walls and towers that survived the onslaughts of centuries. From the surrounding walls, you can see two well preserved underground rooms, one sanctuary, a cistern and five *talayots*. Talayots are large structures made of stone up to nine meters high. They are not quite unlike the pyramids we have come to know.

Son Catlar is but a short drive from Ciutadella, and is surrounded by some of the best sunbathing beaches on the island, including Cala des Talajer and Cala Macarella.

## 🌑 Torretrencada

Another prehistoric settlement is only seven kilometers outside Ciutadella.

Indeed, every historic settlement and every ruined town has something unique to offer travelers. At Torretrencada, you will find some of the biggest and impressive *tuala* on the island.

Tuales, meaning tables in the local dialect, are large blocks of limestone, resting on one other and carefully jointed to resemble a massive altar. Some of these tuales can weigh up to 25 tons, so this sheer engineering feat speaks of the incredible skill of their makers.

Interestingly, tuales are always found in an enclosure of other smaller buildings or constructions. The taules here are surrounded by a series of other structures, from burial caves to stone huts remnants.

## 🌍 San Agueda Castle

Found in the Ferreries district, San Agueda Castle was erected in the 1200's on its namesake plateau. The San Agueda hill is the third highest point on the island at 264 meters above sea-level, and it is this unobscured vantage point that made the castle a well defended fortress. It was the only stronghold to protect the island from northern invasions, and it was so successful in holding its ground that it was the last place to fall during the invasion by Alfonso III.

A rugged but still largely intact Roman Road leads up the castle where histories and cultures collide. And just like

## **MENORCA TRAVEL GUIDE**

any castle worth its name, San Agueda is shrouded in myth and legend. If you are superstitious, beware.

It is said that the hill is haunted and covered in magical holes and magical traps from which you will never escape

# MENORCA TRAVEL GUIDE

## Budget Tips

# 🌍 Accommodation

Travelling to a Mediterranean paradise like Menorca can easily strain your budget when you are looking for a suitable hotel or decent lodgings. Luckily, there are quite a few privately owned comfortable hotels that won't burn through your spendings. Also don't exclude the option of private apartments and holiday homes. Often, the weekly

# MENORCA TRAVEL GUIDE

rate per unit will work out much cheaper than a per person rate at a luxury hotel.

## Hotel Mar Blava

Calle Avenida Del Mar 16, Ciutadella

0203 027 9779

http://www.hostelbookers.com/hostels/spain/menorca/58222/

From €57 per night

Mar Blava is small intimate hotel with only 18 guestrooms, and is located in a prime location in Ciudadella. Painted in a bright pink, the hotel is hard to miss. Overlooking the water and a quiet inlet, the views are simply lovely. It is literally within walking distance of the nearest beach, with quick and easy access to the Cathedral Menorca. It is the

## MENORCA TRAVEL GUIDE

ideal location for travellers who wish to explore the area on foot.

The hotel features a bar that overlooks the swimming pool, a restaurant and a rooftop terrace with views over the inlet, and complimentary Wi-Fi. The terrace steps give you easy access for swimming and snorkelling in the clear blue water below.

The continental breakfast includes an adequate selection of cereals, cheese, cold meats and preserves to kick start your day.

Staff are discreet and very friendly and will even assist you with planning your itinerary and tour bookings.

**MENORCA TRAVEL GUIDE**

## Hotel Hesperia Menorca Patricia

Paseo San Nicolas 90-92, Ciutadella

+34 971 385 511

http://www.hesperia.com/nh/en/hotels/spain/menorca/hesperia-patricia.html

From € 38 per night

Hotel Hesperia is located right next to the picturesque harbour in the historical Ciutadella. It boasts stunning views of the coast and Mediterranean Ocean, where guest can explore the many coves hidden along the shoreline, or take a refreshing dip in the sparkling clear water.

This homey hotel offers air conditioner in all the public places, but a soft sea breeze rolling in from the harbour is equally refreshing. The hotel has recently been refurbished, adding to the comfort of your stay. Bedrooms are spacious and modern, and there is a library on site, with a selection of English literature.

The swimming pool is the perfect place to sip on scrumptious cocktails while lazing in a deck chair as you soak up the sun. From its central location, you can easily explore the beautiful and historical old town on foot. The restaurant serves the three main meals a day, with an extensive children menu for the young ones.

## Apartamentos Roc Lago Park

Calle Alisos s/n Cala'n Bosch, Ciutadella
+44 203 027 7155
http://www.venere.com/vacation-rentals/ciudadela/vacation-rental-roc-lago-park/
From € 27 per person per night

Roc Lago Park is offers holiday rentals comprised of various bungalows and self catering apartments in true Spanish style.

It is conveniently close to Ciutadella's city center and the sandy beaches of Cala en Bosch.

There is a wide selection of water sport excursions to pick and choose from close by, along with lively bars and an extensive entertainment program from young and old alike. There are two large outdoor swimming pools surrounded by a solarium, where you can simply can back and soak up the sun.

## Hotel Globales Almirante Farragut

Urbanizacion Los Delfines, Ciutadella
01 65 69 437
http://www.hotelesglobales.com/en/club-hotel-almirante-farragut-cala-n-forcat-ciutadella-menorca.html?src=af
From €36 per night

When it comes to views and the convenience of a selection of facilities, Almirante Farragut is an excellent choice. Perched on a cliff in Cala n Forcat a short distance from the city center, the hotel overlooks the bay and inlet, providing guests with a view that is simply magnificent.

At an all inclusive package, the hotel offers excellent value for money. You will find a complete buffet in the main dining room, and there is a very spacious lounge and a few bars.

To keep guests thoroughly entertained between excursions, there are two salt water swimming pools, table tennis rooms, a tennis court, a mini club for the young ones and a variety of life shows for young and old alike. The hotel even has its very own discothèque on the grounds.

## Hostal Jume

Concepción, 6, 07701 Mahón
+34 971 363 266
http://www.hostaljume.com/
info@hostaljume.com
From €18 per night

# MENORCA TRAVEL GUIDE

Hostal Jume is more like a guest house than a hostel, with private en-suite bathrooms and air conditioners in the rooms. It is spotlessly clean with excellent staff on hand, who provide you with fresh sheets and towels on a daily basis.

There are 39 guest rooms in total, and you can choose between single, double or quadruple rooms. The décor is simply, yet bright and airy, and continental breakfast is served in the on-site café with bread still warm from the bakery. For the price, you will be hard pressed to find lodgings of similar standards within city.

It is set in old town, and is a ten minute walk from the Santa Maria Church and Plaza de Conquesta. Jume is only 200 meters from the famous Mahon port, and guest are within walking distance of multitude of restaurants and lively bars, with the nearest beach six kilometers away.

In spite of its central location in one of the livelier parts of town, Jume is on a small quiet street across from the police station, so guest can be assured of peace and quiet when they return after an eventful day.

## 🌎 Shopping

Because Menorca is more traditional and laid back than its neighbouring islands, you shouldn't expect to do much shopping out of town, with the exception of local markets.

There are not many international chain stores here, but think of this a way to truly appreciate the local quality crafts and souvenirs.

As there are no large shopping malls, shopping is overall relaxed at a leisurely pace. Here you will only find truly unique little boutiques, so there is no repetitive shops like the mass chain stores back home.

Both Mahon and Ciutadella have fantastic open air arts and craft markets every weekend that sells a wide selection of goodies, from unique pieces of clothing to memorable souvenirs. It is worth mentioning that if you

# MENORCA TRAVEL GUIDE

are planning to shop on a budget, it is best to avoid Ciutadella's old town, as the prices here tend to be a little more in the high end designer category

Don't forget about the customary siesta times when you plan a shopping excursion. Usually shops close between 13.30 and 16.30 pm.

## Castillo Menorca

7 Kilometers outside Ciutadella
Open between May and October from 10.00 am to 19.00 pm.

Castillo is one of the few outlet stores on the western part of the island, where you will find a few branded goods at reasonable prices and basic souvenirs. Also on offer is a fine selection of leather goods, jewellery and ceramics. The entertainment area makes this the perfect shopping and entertainment park for the entire family.

## Mercat de Claustre

Mahon Center, Clost to Carmen Church
Monday to Saturday

Markets are the best places if you are looking for a bargain, and Mercat de Claustre is no exception. The market is housed inside what used to be the convent of Carme Cloister in the 1700's. Traders have already occupied this space for over a century. On the ground floor, you will find a selection of fresh produce, but a new addition to building added a brand new commercial space.

Here you will find a whole selection of shops that sells anything from flowers to shoes. The market provides for a great day out, and during the summer months, many cultural events and life entertainment takes place in the cloister's central space.

# Centro Artesanal

Es Mercadal

Centro Artesanal in Es Mercadal town is the meeting place for artists where they can promote both modern and traditional pieces. It also showcases a wide variety of ancient trades that are still in practise to this day. This includes silversmiths, tapestry weavers and even bee keepers.

All the products can be purchased directly at the shop on the premises. Handcrafted silverware can be rather costly but goods on display can usually meet every budget. When visiting the centre, don't miss the opportunity to see master craftsman Arturo work his magic on ceramics the traditional way. A fired clay milk jug will make a great souvenir to take back home.

# MENORCA TRAVEL GUIDE

## Bangels Accessories

Calle Angel 25, Mahon

971 354 724

As their slogan states, Bangles adds sparkles to the Mahon fashion scene. They sell an exclusive collection of well made and decently priced costume jewelry, handbags, scarves and a selection of unique accessories to prep up an old outfit.

It is a great place to shop for take-home gifts for friends and family, and your purchases will be beautifully wrapped to save you the trouble. It is also the only shop on the entire island to stock Shamballas crystal jewelry. These stylish "bling" is almost blinding in its luster.

## Arts & Crafts Markets

There is no better place to find a true bargain than at an outdoor market, and luckily for you, Menorca is crawling with markets. Crawling, literally, since many of the markets belong to travelling merchants, just like times of old.

When it comes to flea market hopping, you are really spoiled for choice. Some of the most popular markets in Mahon include:

- Mercat Ambulant De S'Esplanada selling textiles and decorative goods. This market is known for travelling around.

- Mercat Ambulant del Parc Rochina stock various goods from good quality T-shirts to leather goods.

- Mercat Artesa de Mahon offers handmade goods and works of art.

# 🌐 Places to Eat

Eating out on a daily basis will also cost you a pretty penny and leave a hole in your pocket before you know it. Nothing is to say that you can not enjoy a daily meal in comfort at one of the many local hideouts, but the trick is to do it so wisely. Breakfast actually consist of two parts; an early morning refreshment of preserves and milky coffee, and mid morning breakfast, which is more substantial.

If you've opted for staying in a hotel, at least one of your daily meals will be included in the price. However, if you've gone the self-catering route, both cities, Mahon and Ciutadelle offer fabulous fresh food markets right in the town centers. You will also find that many restaurants and cafés offer excellent lunchtime specials.

## La Minerva

Moll del Llevant 87, Mahon
97 135 1995
Main courses start at €18

# MENORCA TRAVEL GUIDE

Reservations required

If you like seafood, you are in for a real treat at La Minerva. It is one of Mahon's finest, and located right in the port, it is everything you will expect from an authentically Spanish eatery. The atmosphere is warm and cosy, with a mouthwatering selection of clams, mussels and lobster. For the meat lovers, there is a selection of succulent meat dishes on the menu as well, including pork loin with a plumb sauce, and mini meatballs dipped in almond sauce. In true fashion of the Med, the food is very aromatic and flavourful

The décor is relatively simple with a nautical flair and views over the harbour. All the main meals are prepared in the building across the road, and it is quite amusing to see skilled waiters dash between buildings while avoiding traffic.

## Bar Restaurant España

Carrer Victori 48-50, Mahon
97 136 3299

Main Course starts at €14

Reservations are recommended, but not required

This is one of the longest continuing restaurants since it opened its doors in 1938; no small feat in this industry. The success of Espana is mostly due to the hearty portions at a very reasonable price, and a steady flow of loyal and supporting patrons. This is the place to be if you wish to rub shoulders with locals and holiday goers alike as you while away an evening in conversation.

The menu is varied to appeal to mostly everyone while naturally maintaining its distinct Spanish flair. You can expect a wide selection of seafood dishes, which will include the catch of the day, as well as meaty meals of steak, veal and pork.

## Restaurante Ca Na Marga

Urb. Ses Salines n.1, Fornells

971376410

Main courses from €10

Reservations are recommended.

# MENORCA TRAVEL GUIDE

Located just off the Fornells highway, this family owned restaurant is unpretentious, with the sole focus on delectable food. Ca Na Marga prides itself on its authenticity, and man size steaks are cooked in the open grill in the centre of the dining room. Make no mistake; the steaks are as massive as they are succulent.

Pizzas made the traditional way are at the order of the day, but the menu is varied with a decent mixed selection.

The setting is completely casual, and there is no dress code, so it is the ideal place to stop for a bite after a long day.

## Cafe Balear

Passeig Pla de Sant Joan 15, Ciutadella
+34 97 138 00 05
Main courses from €20

For over 30 years, this little piece of culinary heaven in the port of the city has been serving fresh fish caught daily by their very own boat. With main courses starting at €20 it is not the cheapest restaurant around, but it is one of the best rated restaurants in Menorca, famous for the seafood. The portions are generous, and the quality of the food is practically unsurpassable.

Aside from seafood, there is an extensive menu, with interesting dishes like the signature lobster casserole. All the desserts are home made, and the personal touch of the establishment does not go unnoticed.

## La Cayena

Alaior 40, Ciutadella
971 482 212
Main courses from €8

The white washed house and the intimate interior courtyard at La Cayena will make patrons feel right at home. You can choose from an exotic menu in a very relaxed but cheerful atmosphere. The restaurant even has a selection of burgers available, something that seems to be scarcity in Menorca. If burgers are not exotic enough,

## **MENORCA TRAVEL GUIDE**

the menu is further comprised of Mexican fajitas, salads, Thai and Indonesian fusion dishes, and Japanese. When you've had your fill of Mediterranean food, La Cayena is one of the best places to satisfy your taste for international cuisine.

# MENORCA TRAVEL GUIDE

## Know Before You Go

## 🌐 Entry Requirements

By virtue of the Schengen agreement, visitors from other countries in the European Union will not need a visa when visiting Spain. Additionally visitors from Switzerland, Norway, Lichtenstein, Iceland, Canada, the United Kingdom, Australia and the USA are also exempt. Independently travelling minors will need to carry written permission from their parents. If visiting from a country where you require a visa to enter Spain, you will also need to state the purpose of your visit and provide proof that you have financial means to support yourself for the duration of your stay. Unless you are an EU national, your passport should be valid for at least 3 months after the end of your stay.

## 🌐 Health Insurance

Citizens of other EU countries are covered for emergency health care in Spain. UK residents, as well as visitors from Switzerland are covered by the European Health Insurance Card (EHIC), which can be applied for free of charge. Visitors from non-Schengen countries will need to show proof of private health insurance that is valid for the duration of their stay in Spain, as part of their visa application.

## 🌐 Travelling with Pets

Spain participates in the Pet Travel Scheme (PETS) which allows UK residents to travel with their pets without requiring quarantine upon re-entry. Certain conditions will need to be met. The animal will have to be microchipped and up to date on rabies vaccinations. Additionally, you will need a PETS re-entry certificate issued by a UK vet, an Export Health Certificate (this is required by the Spanish authorities), an official Certificate of Treatment against dangerous parasites such as tapeworm and ticks and an official Declaration that your pet has not left the qualifying countries within this period. Pets from the USA or Canada may be brought in under the conditions of a non-commercial import. For this, your pet will also need to be microchipped (or marked with an identifying tattoo) and up to date on rabies vaccinations.

## 🌐 Airports

**Adolfo Suárez Madrid–Barajas Airport** (MAD) is the largest and busiest airport in Spain. It is located about 9km from the financial district of Madrid, the capital. The busiest route is the so-called "Puente Aéreo" or "air bridge", which connects Madrid with Barcelona. The second busiest airport in Spain is **Barcelona–El Prat Airport** (BCN), located about 14km southwest from the center of Barcelona. There are two terminals. The newer Terminal 1 handles the bulk of its traffic, while the older Terminal 2 is used by budget airlines such as EasyJet.

**Palma de Mallorca Airport** (PMI) is the third largest airport in Spain and one of its busiest in the summer time. It has the capacity of processing 25 million passengers annually. **Gran Canaria Airport** (LPA) handles around 10 million passengers annually and connects travellers with the Canary Islands. **Pablo Ruiz Picasso Malaga Airport** (AGP) provides access to the Costa del Sol. Other southern airports are **Seville Airport** (SVQ), **Jaen Federico Garcia Lorca Airport** (GRX) near Granada, **Jerez de la Frontera Airport**, which connects travellers to Costa del Luz and Cadiz and **Almeria Airport** (LEI).

## 🌍 Airlines

Iberia is the flag carrying national airline of Spain. Since a merger in 2010 with British Airways, it is part of the International Airlines Group (IAG). Iberia is in partnership with the regional carrier Air Nostrum and Iberia Express, which

# MENORCA TRAVEL GUIDE

focusses on medium and short haul routes. Vueling is a low-cost Spanish airline with connections to over 100 destinations. In partnership with MTV, it also provides a seasonal connection to Ibiza. Volotea is a budget airline based in Barcelona, which mainly flies to European destinations. Air Europe, the third largest airline after Iberia and Vueling connects Europe to resorts in the Canaries and the Balearic Islands and also flies to North and South America. Swiftair flies mainly to destinations in Europe, North Africa and the Middle East.

Barcelona-El Prat Airport serves as a primary hub for Iberia Regional. It is also a hub for Vueling. Additionally it functions as a regional hub for Ryanair. Air Europe's primary hubs are at Palma de Mallorca Airport and Madrid Barajas Airport, but other bases are at Barcelona Airport and Tenerife South Airport. Air Nostrum is served by hubs at Barcelona Airport, Madrid Barajas Airport and Valencia Airport. Gran Canaria Airport is the hub for the regional airline, Binter Canarias.

## 🌐 Currency

Spain's currency is the Euro. It is issued in notes in denominations of €500, €200, €100, €50, €20, €10 and €5. Coins are issued in denominations of €2, €1, 50c, 20c, 10c, 5c, 2c and 1c.

# MENORCA TRAVEL GUIDE

## 🌐 Banking & ATMs

You should have no trouble making withdrawals in Spain if your ATM card is compatible with the MasterCard/Cirrus or Visa/Plus networks. If you want to save money, avoid using the dynamic currency conversion (DCC) system, which promises to charge you in your own currency for the Euros you withdraw. The fine print is that your rate will be less favorable. Whenever possible, opt to conduct your transaction in Euros instead. Do remember to advise your bank or credit card company of your travel plans before leaving.

## 🌐 Credit Cards

Visa and MasterCard will be accepted at most outlets that handle credit cards in Spain, but you may find that your American Express card is not as welcome at all establishments. While shops may still be able to accept transactions with older magnetic strip cards, you will need a PIN enabled card for transactions at automatic vendors such as ticket sellers. Do not be offended when asked to show proof of ID when paying by credit card. It is common practice in Spain and Spaniards are required by law to carry identification on them at all times.

# MENORCA TRAVEL GUIDE

## 🌐 Tourist Taxes

In the region of Catalonia, which includes Barcelona, a tourist tax of between €0.45 and €2.50 per night is levied for the first seven days of your stay. The amount depends on the standard of the establishment, but includes youth hostels, campgrounds, holiday apartments and cruise ships with a stay that exceeds 12 hours.

## 🌐 Reclaiming VAT

If you are not from the European Union, you can claim back VAT (or Value Added Tax) paid on your purchases in Spain. The VAT rate in Spain is 18 percent. VAT refunds are made on purchases of €90.15 and over from a single shop. Look for shops displaying Global Blue Tax Free Shopping signage. You will be required to fill in a form at the shop, which must then be stamped at the Customs office at the airport. Customs officers will want to inspect your purchases to make sure that they are sealed and unused. Once this is done, you will be able to claim your refund from the Refund Office at the airport. Alternately, you can mail the form to Global Blue once you get home for a refund on your credit card.

# MENORCA TRAVEL GUIDE

## 🌐 Tipping policy

In general, Spain does not really have much of a tipping culture and the Spanish are not huge tippers themselves. When in a restaurant, check your bill to see whether a gratuity is already included. If not, the acceptable amount will depend on the size of the meal, the prestige of the restaurant and the time of day. For a quick coffee, you can simply round the amount off. For lunch in a modest establishment, opt for 5 percent or one euro per person. The recommended tip for dinner would be more generous, usually somewhere between 7 and 10 percent. This will depend on the type of establishment.

In hotels, if there is someone to help you with your luggage, a tip of 1 euro should be sufficient. At railway stations and airports, a tip is not really expected. Rounding off the amount of the fare to the nearest euro would be sufficient for a taxi driver. If you recruited a private driver, you may wish to tip that person at the end of your association with him.

## 🌐 Mobile Phones

Most EU countries, including Spain uses the GSM mobile service. This means that most UK phones and some US and Canadian phones and mobile devices will work in Spain. While you could check with your service provider about coverage before you leave, using your own service in roaming mode will involve additional costs. The alternative is to purchase a Spanish SIM card to use during your stay in Spain.

Spain has four mobile networks. They are Movistar, Vodafone, Orange and Yoiga. Buying a Spanish SIM card is relatively simple and inexpensive. By law, you will be required to show some form of identification such as a passport. A basic SIM card from Vodafone costs €5. There are two tourist packages available for €15, which offers a combination of 1Gb data, together with local and international call time. Alternately, a data only package can also be bought for €15. From Orange, you can get a SIM card for free, with a minimum top-up purchase of €10. A tourist SIM with a combination of data and voice calls can be bought for €15. Movistar offers a start-up deal of €10. At their sub-branches, Tuenti, you can also get a free SIM, but the catch is that you need to choose a package to get it. The start-up cost at Yoiga is €20.

## 🌏 Dialling Code

The international dialling code for Spain is +34.

# MENORCA TRAVEL GUIDE

## 🌐 Emergency Numbers

All Emergencies: 112 (no area code required)

Police (municipal): 092

Police (national): 091

Police (tourist police, Madrid): 91 548 85 37

Police (tourist police, Barcelona): 93 290 33 27

Ambulance: 061 or 112

Fire: 080 or 112

Traffic: 900 123 505

Electricity: 900 248 248

Immigration: 900 150 000

MasterCard: 900 958 973

Visa: 900 99 1124

## 🌐 Public Holidays

1 January: New Year's Day (Año Nuevo)

6 January: Day of the Epiphany/Three Kings Day (Reyes Mago)

March/April: Good Friday

1 May: Labor Day (Día del Trabajo)

15 August: Assumption of Mary (Asunción de la Virgen)

12 October: National Day of Spain/Columbus Day (Fiesta Nacional de España or Día de la Hispanidad)

# MENORCA TRAVEL GUIDE

1 November: All Saints Day (Fiesta de Todos los Santos)

6 December: Spanish Constitution Day (Día de la Constitución)

8 December: Immaculate Conception (La Immaculada)

25 December: Christmas (Navidad)

Easter Monday is celebrated in the Basque region, Castile-La Mancha, Catalonia, La Rioja, Navarra and Valencia. 26 December is celebrated as Saint Stephen's Day in Catalonia and the Balearic Islands.

## 🌐 Time Zone

Spain falls in the Central European Time Zone. This can be calculated as Greenwich Mean Time/Co-ordinated Universal Time (GMT/UTC) +2; Eastern Standard Time (North America) -6; Pacific Standard Time (North America) -9.

## 🌐 Daylight Savings Time

Clocks are set forward one hour on the last Sunday in March and set back one hour on the last Sunday in October for Daylight Savings Time.

# MENORCA TRAVEL GUIDE

## 🌎 School Holidays

Spain's academic year is from mid-September to mid-June. It is divided into three terms with two short breaks of about two weeks around Christmas and Easter.

## 🌎 Trading Hours

Trading hours in Spain usually run from 9.30am to 1.30pm and from 4.30pm to 8pm, from Mondays to Saturdays. Malls and shopping centers often trade from 10am to 9pm without closing. During the peak holiday seasons, shops could stay open until 10pm. Lunch is usually served between 1pm and 3.30pm while dinner is served from 8.30 to 11pm.

## 🌎 Driving Laws

The Spanish drive on the right hand side of the road. You will need a driver's licence which is valid in the EC to be able to hire a car in Spain. The legal driving age is 18, but most rental companies will require you to be at least 21 to be able to rent a car. You will need to carry your insurance documentation and rental contract with you at all times, when driving. The speed limit in Spain is 120km per hour on motorways, 100km per hour on dual carriageways and 90km per hour on single carriageways. Bear in mind that it is illegal to drive in Spain wearing sandals or flip-flops.

You may drive a non-Spanish vehicle in Spain provided that it is considered roadworthy in the country where it is registered. As a UK resident, you will be able to drive a vehicle registered in the UK in Spain for up to six months, provided that your liabilities as a UK motorist, such as MOT, road tax and insurance are up to date for the entire period of your stay. The legal limit in Spain is 0.05, but for new drivers who have had their licence for less than two years, it is 0.03.

## 🌎 Drinking Laws

In Spain, the minimum drinking age is 18. Drinking in public places is forbidden and can be punished with a spot fine. In areas where binge drinking can be a problem, alcohol trading hours are often limited.

## 🌎 Smoking Laws

In the beginning of 2006, Spain implemented a policy banning smoking from all public and private work places. This includes schools, libraries, museums, stadiums, hospitals, cinemas, theatres and shopping centers as well as public transport. From 2011, smoking was also banned in restaurants and bars, although designated smoking areas can be created provided they are enclosed and well ventilated. Additionally tobacco products may only be sold from tobacconists and bars and restaurants where smoking is permitted. Smoking near children's parks, schools or health centers carries a €600 fine.

## 🌐 Electricity

Electricity: 220 volts

Frequency: 50 Hz

Your electrical appliances from the UK and Ireland should be able to function sufficiently in Spain, but since Spain uses 2 pin sockets, you will need a C/F adapter to convert the plug from 3 to 2-pins. The voltage and frequency is compatible with UK appliances. If travelling from the USA, you will need a converter or step-down transformer to convert your appliances to 110 volts. The latest models of many laptops, camcorders, cell phones and digital cameras are dual-voltage with a built in converter.

## 🌐 Food & Drink

Spanish cuisine is heavily influenced by a Moorish past. Staple dishes include the rice dish, Paella, Jamon Serrano (or Spanish ham), Gazpacho (cold tomato-based vegetable soup), roast suckling pig, chorizo (spicy sausage) and the Spanish omelette. Tapas (hot or cold snacks) are served with drinks in Spanish bars.

The most quintessentially Spanish drink is sangria, but a popular alternative with the locals is tinto de verano, or summer wine, a mix of red wine and lemonade. Vino Tinto or red wine compliments most meal choices. The preferred red grape type is Tempranillo, for which the regions of Roija and Ribera del Duero are famous. A well-known sparkling wine, Cava, is grown in Catalonia. Do try the Rebujito, a Seville style mix of sherry, sparkling water and mint. The most popular local beers are Cruzcampo, Alhambra and Estrello Damm. Coffee is also popular with Spaniards, who prefer Café con leche (espresso with milk).

# Websites

http://www.idealspain.com
A detailed resource that includes legal information for anyone planning a longer stay or residency in Spain.
http://spainattractions.es/
http://www.tourspain.org/
http://spainguides.com/
http://www.travelinginspain.com/
http://wikitravel.org/en/Spain

# **MENORCA TRAVEL GUIDE**

Printed in Great Britain
by Amazon